Amusablue

Pui Man Wong

BookLeaf Publishing

India | USA | UK

Presentation by *BookLeaf Publishing*

Web: www.bookleafpub.com

E-mail: info@bookleafpub.com

ISBN : 9789357611817

First edition 2021

ACKNOWLEDGEMENT

I'd like to thank my parents, Simon and Annie. Thank you for taking good care of me and tolerating the mood swings of their 'emo kid'.

I really want to thank my friends who have been supporting me through difficult times. Wendy Chan, Gwyneth Au, Y.T. Ching and Yeeman-thank you for reminding me I am much stronger than I thought and encouraging me to be who I want to be. You have taught me the importance to live, rather than just exist. I doubt if I would explore the possibility and establish @amusablue.poetry in the first place without you guys. Really grateful to have Wendy and Gwyn who proofread my work.

Thank you for the BookLeaf Publishing who held the campaign to help aspiring writers to achieve their goals.

Finally, thanks for everyone who read this book and support @amusablue.poetry on Instagram. It means the world to me!

The End

Mistake after mistake,
The famous star-crossed lovers from
Shakespeare's could never escape from death.
People consider it a tragedy over the centuries
and pity Romeo and Juliet's with their miserable
end.
But the destined death is where their story truly
begins.

The curtains gradually close
along with the applause from the audience,
They leave the auditorium, realising the sunset
has already gone
and replaced by the shimmering stars.
Tears and laughter may remain within the
theatre, yet once the show ends,
we certainly do not realise that we will never be
the same person again.

Involved in the ceaseless wheel,
We are all fools in Time as he never ever tries to
explain when the event begins.
Hence, we mistreat winter with mortal terror,
and praise spring with all the blossoming glory.
If the leaves do not fall, do you seriously believe

the flowers would ever burgeon at all?

Therefore, as a journey starts, let's begin with 'The End'.

Into the Water

If you don't ever have the courage
to dive into the water,
you will
never
able to feel its tenderness.

To the Lighthouse

From the day you have gone,
I drowned in the water,
faced the thunders
alone.
Hope that one day
I will reach the lighthouse guiding me
to the shore.

Be Brave

Sometimes you may not born
with a heart of the pirate,
You have to be one
when you're already sailing in the ocean.

When the Poet isn't Ready to Write,

Part 1

Poets are so emotion-driven.
You'd better let a poet write when they want to,
rather than ask them to write.

"Apple"
Write about apple.
I write about apple because they love apple.
I write about apple because they love apple, yet I
have never been a fan of apple.
I won't write about apple because they ADORE
apple.
I certainly hate apple.
"Apple"

So only the title "Apple" is written
on the last piece of paper.
That's everything I could write
at the moment.

The Subtle Defiance

A rose is a rose is a rose.
(Your name) is (Your name) is (Your name).

The bully is excited to explore the edge of your
vulnerability.
You are resorted to defeat the sense of your
authenticity.

Do not compromise or flinch.
Slap their faces by living the best version of
your life
with confidence. That's the best vengeance.

The Degrading of
Love

Love was an ability,
yet we distorted it
as vulnerability
in modern day.

Our Fading Summer

Our love is a summer ecstasy.
All wonderful except
it's now autumn.

When the Poet is enthusiastic in writing about Something,

Part 2

Poets are so emotion-driven.
Once they start transforming their idea into words,
they are no longer in the same world.

"Apple"

People always misinterpret the forbidden fruit to be an apple,
but why not as long as it can be the symbol of enticement
from the famous fallen angel
in the story of human fall.

Just because of a tiny bite of the forbidden apple,
We lost the paradise. Yet we cannot blame Eve.
That was certainly irresistible,

especially with the rules God enforced,
though only Eve might be adrift.

That was a choice to be made,
Even if the serpent did not invade.
Eve would only be Adam's rib,
playing an unfair game she would never win.

Now even the Story of the Fall is referenced
under the title of "Apple",
which could be expanded with a few more
pages.
So maybe we just let the poet continue to weave
his thoughts
into the poem.

The Modern Masquerade

No more paper faces on parade,
nor people in disguise dancing in the palace.
Masks, grand mansions and guests are all
replaced,
the 17th century landlords would certainly be
amazed.

Foundations, eye shadows and lipsticks are all
you need.
Take selfies with several selected filters and
create a Boomerage.
A cliché caption and some hashtags like #ootd
and #moodoftoday.
That's how we do our masquerade nowadays.

Firework

We shined and vanished,
as if the fireworks burst in the air.
But at least we stole
that moment of glitter.

The Pre-metamorphosis Period

I've never thought of what I would become
when I was in the dark,
where only the shadows lasted.

Not a glimpse of the gleaming light,
how could I be hopeful during these unendurable
nights?
The sun used to guide me was gone.
Nothing remained.
The mystery bothered me.
The uncertainty manipulated me.
The fear engulfed me.

However an inspiration came to me when I was
mourning for my previous life,
that everything would always come to an end.
Let's be patient and burgeon.
Hopefully I will find the tiny hole in my
chrysalis.

Wandering in the Literal Labyrinth

I walked into several bookstores
when I was in France alone.
With my limited knowledge of French, I tried to
find,
to find the book that defines us lastly.

My 1st Priority Nowadays

Not because I am tired
of loving you,
just that I love myself
more than you now.

The Haunted House

The darkness consumes me again,
the demon revisits repeatedly, always with an
inescapable attack,
I doubt if I still exist.
I lay down on my bed for a while as I can barely
move.
Yet I don't sleep, can't sleep,
Insomnia is one of my best friends.

Sometimes I wonder if I still
breathe, being too unmotivated that
I probably live much worse than the walking
dead.
Believing that I will be laying on my deathbed
soon
quietly and motionlessly.

All the world is in a B/W filter which I can
never detach.
I am not sure if I like to remove the tinted
glasses,
so beautifully miserable,
these melancholies are the sorrow I swallowed.
I do not concern where the colours have gone,

the fact is that they are all gone.
The level of codependency is beyond my control
already.
Drowning into the deep ocean seems to be my
only remedy.

Pain, the feeling I no longer feel,
the last sensation which I used to perceive is
gone too.
Forever.
The numbness deludes me that my heart does
not ache,
even though I am consciously aware that
I keep experiencing these ceaseless heart attacks.
As if a huge hole has been punched through my
heart,
A hole that leads to no end.

I am no more than a haunted house, a haunted
house without a ghost.
People say that I would be better after shrieking.
I don't know what I can respond
while I am crying every second already,
just there is no tear.

Maybe I should be grateful that
at least there is still a part of me
desiring to get rid of this haunted house.
Maybe that day will come soon,

hopefully before I die.

The Delicate Sweetness

Your soft gaze matches the colour of dawn
in that seemingly endless morning.
In that lazy Saturday morning,
all sophistications have gone
and only two unarmed hopeless romantics.

Interpretation of a Stunning Smile

I love seeing the eye wrinkles in your smile.
They see your wrinkles as the defect of ageing,
Yet for me it's the sincerity of your sensation.

The Lost Courage

Little Cubic bestows me with his love arrow,
I wonder if the angel with broken wings
could thoroughly perform the magic.

The Sedation

Inebriated in laudanum,
fill yourself with haze
to get out of the maze,
striving to obliviate
the pseudo-romantic monological melodrama.

Finding Unicorn

I am a unicorn
in waiting of
another unicorn.

The Start

I hold that fragile dandelion clock with
numerous seeds
and ask the wind for a favour.
The time comes as the breeze blows.
I blow too, as a blessing for these little
adventurers to start their lives.
I bury the withered beauty in my hand and sing a
cheerful sweet elegy.

Whispering goodbye to the meadow we used to
spend time in,
This will be the last time I come back.
He has vanished in my life for years.
Gazing at the place,
I cannot help myself from reminiscence.
My tears are rolling down my cheeks freely,
I am determined to stop lingering in the past
and be fearless to live in the present.

As if the whisper of goodbye isn't enough,
Adieu. Adieu. All my sorrows and the past!
Release the misery and happiness lasts.
A bright new future I'm going to start.
I yell this out loud with my cracking voice
and leave.

A smile appears under my swollen, yet smiley
eyes.

The inherent reluctance about closure prevents
us from moving forward,
Yet each moment is precious only because of its
temporary existence.
Moving on with courage is the turning point for
growth,
embrace the uncertain future full of possibilities.
Let's end here with 'The Start' and venture into
the new journey.